Three Key Marketing Strategies

What We Can Learn from Instagram's
Enormous Success

Mark Weber
Sunbird Marketing

Table of Contents

Introduction 1

The Rise of Instagram – Background on the Founders 3

The Creation of Burbn.. 4

How Burbn Became Instagram 6

The Three Principles...7

The First Filters 9

Instagram Immediate Hit Upon Launching 10

The Decision to Sell to Facebook 12

A Continuous Growth...14

Timeless Marketing Strategies..16

Marketing Strategy 1: Focus on What People Want and Say – Listen for Demand 17

The Importance of Feedback and Data Analysis 17

The Market Research...19

What Instagram Did 20

Methods to Get Quality Feedback from Your Customers or Users...22

The Voice of People Is Important............................ 25

Marketing Strategy 2: Solve a Real Problem – Fill the Demand – Supply... 26

Basic Steps to Solve a Problem and Fill Demand 26

Other Instagram Strategies to Solve a Problem and Fill the Demand 31

Marketing Strategy 3: Launch Small and Develop Based on Feedback.. 37

Launching Small vs. Launching Big 38

What Happens Once You Spike?................................ 39

The Post-Launch Feedback 41

Conclusion.. 44

Introduction

What's the first thing someone does immediately after waking up? When asked, people would either say that they go wash their faces, brush their teeth, and other similar "morning activities." In truth, however, there is one thing that we all do before anything else: grab our phones. And when we do that, out of instinct, we check social media – which most of the time, is Instagram.

In a way, you could say that Instagram is the modern equivalent of a cave wall. Cavemen painted the walls of their caves in order to communicate with each other, to decorate their walls, to express their feelings and to show that they are actually doing something. Now read all that out loud, and try to apply it to Instagram: looks to be pretty much the same thing, right?

Enter the 21st century, when the world saw the creation of Instagram – which wasn't even called Instagram. In the beginning, it was Burbn – a project that two bright men were working on. The idea hit them randomly – mainly as they were practicing their coding skills. Most of the work was done on their free time – and with no actual plan for the future regarding its success. It was more of a "let's see if it works kind of project."

It didn't work – or did it? Needless to say, Burbn had a pretty great role in creating what we know today as Instagram. Many would say that it was a lucky break – one we never actually thought would happen. It was one of those happy accidents that started with two people simply meeting up, saying "hey, let's try this."

Now, look at Instagram. Having around 1 billion active users everywhere, it follows just after Facebook and YouTube in terms of popularity. Around 99.9% of those that have a social life have Instagram – and the rest are the kind that avoids all types of social media altogether.

So, how did it manage to turn from a failed project into one that has so many active users? It's kind of hard to believe that something that failed so bad can become so successful. Well, British scholar C. S. Lewis once said that "Failures are finger posts on the road to achievement" – and in a way, it makes sense. By failing, we learn exactly what went wrong – and what we have to do in order to make it right.

Is this what the creators of Instagram did? Well, it seems so. Needless to say, compared to its inexistent popularity in the past, now it's like you don't exist if you don't have Instagram. And all of this thanks to the strategies they implemented.

By reading this book, you can find out what those strategies are and what you can learn from them for your own projects. It is a story of how Instagram rose to success, despite its setbacks. It is also a story of what they did to hang onto their success. If you've been using Instagram until now, it is likely that you also want to find out.

The Rise of Instagram – Background on the Founders

Instagram today is one of the largest social media platforms that we have – and with each day, it keeps growing in users and posts. The first prototypes of Instagram were not precisely that popular – but when it had its official launch, the entire thing was like a "boom."

It's difficult to imagine that when the two founders, Kevin Systrom and Mike Krieger met, it was just a stroke of good luck and chance. The two met through the Stanford's Mayfield Fellows Program, where Krieger was studying symbolic systems and Systrom was learning how to code.

Both of them had a love for coding and sharing – so, during their university, they decided to make something out of it. Systrom was deep into the marketing fields during the day – and learning how to code during the night. He came up with a prototype called Burbn – an app that allowed people to check in and be social, without actually having to be social in real life.

This is mostly how he met Krieger as well. Originally, Systrom was a highly enthusiastic Burbn user – but while he knew the app, he did not know Krieger. By chance, both of them participated in the Stanford program, whose purpose was to educate students in entrepreneurship.

They decided to collaborate – and upon the startup of Instagram, their final app already had millions of users. Still, they had to go through the adventure of Burbn first.

The Creation of Burbn

Before there was Instagram, originally there was Burbn. After gaining some knowledge on how to code, Systrom built an HTML prototype that he decided to name Burbn. Why Burbn, you may ask? Well, its name was inspired by one of his loves: fine whiskey and quality bourbon. If you say the app name out loud, you can actually make sense of it.

When it first came out, Burbn was a multi-faceted app that allowed people to create check-ins, share photos and post plans – pretty much like Facebook. He worked on the app during his free evenings and weekends – and a short time later, he had a prototype of this app that he could share with his friends. At first, everything was contained as a personal project created for the fun of it.

However, several weeks later, at a party in Hunch, he came across some seed-stage capital companies, Andreessen Horowitz and Baseline Ventures. These were also Silicon Valley startup firms that wished to personalize social media and the Internet – one phone app at the time.

Systrom gave them a quick demo of his prototype, convincing the companies that they should meet so that they could talk more seriously about Burbn. Two weeks after that meeting happened, Systrom had already raised $500,000 worth of funds and gave up his job to see whether he could turn this app into a reality or not.

This is where Mike Krieger came into the scene. At that point, the two were not exactly friends – but after meeting in San Francisco, they began to exchange tips and hints whenever they would occasionally meet.

Considering that they had a solid idea in mind and that the money was in its place, Krieger jumped in on Systrom's idea of making a business out of Burbn. They made a full version of the app where people could do check-ins, post pictures, and earn points simply for the fact that they were hanging out with friends.

After coming up with a full iOS version and adding a number of features, they decided that Burbn had started to become way too cluttered. It had too much functionality – and while one may think that people would appreciate so many features, most of them would feel overwhelmed by this aspect. It was confusing, and users would practically disappear from the platform and go for other social media apps.

Because of this, they decided that the right step would be to drop the project and start over. They did not see it as a failure; instead, they saw it as an opportunity to do better. And they were right – because this decision of theirs would actually be the step that brought them a global success.

How Burbn Became Instagram

In a way, the problem was that Burbn did not have an actual focus. Like apps such as Foursquare, Burbn allowed you to do many things – to the point where you could feel like it was too much. This is why they decided that some changes were in order – that something had to be done. It became Instagram, a combo word between "instant camera" and "telegram." Unlike Burbn, this one would be more focused on photo sharing rather than on anything else.

According to Krieger, Instagram took about two months until the shipping and building process came to an end – but Systrom says that its initial process lasted for more than a year until it reached success. It was a very detailed project, despite the fact that its purpose here revolved around cameras.

After closing in the $500,000 seed funding with Andreessen Horowitz and Baseline Ventures, Burbn was rebranded into Instagram – gaining new working staff and becoming more and more focused. Josh Riedel became the community manager of the company, Jessica Zollman took on the role of the community evangelist, and Shayne Sweeney became the engineer of the company.

Work has been continuously done on the Instagram app. On October 2006, the iOS app came through the App Store, and people could download and reap the benefits of the app. However, before that, they had a few things to make modifications on, so that Burbn could officially become Instagram.

The Three Principles

To put it simply, there were three principles that they had to work on – and all of them were crucial for success. These principles would "clean" Burbn and make it easier to manage for those that have found the previous application overwhelming.

1. Mobile Photo Quality

When photos were originally uploaded on Burbn, the quality was very bad. The pixels were not doing the pictures any justice – and even a high-quality picture taken with a professional camera would eventually lose its quality. Before it was uploaded, each picture had to be downgraded in order to respect a certain set of dimensions.

To put it simply, when looking at the pictures, you could see that there was too much distance between the picture and the real world. You could see that the photographer wanted to expose the beauty of a certain environment – but the quality of the Burbn picture algorithm would not allow them to do that.

This is why the founders decided that a change was due. If they wanted Instagram to be focused on picture sharing, they had to ensure that the quality of those pictures was up to match. Otherwise, it was no different from any other no-name app you could find on the Internet.

With Instagram, they planned to make it big – to make it as successful as possible. So, they found a new algorithm to help keep the quality of the uploaded pictures. Filters were also used to make viewers feel closers to the pictures that have been uploaded.

2. Ease of Use

Not only was the quality of Burbn pictures very bad, but you also had to go through various troubles to upload a single picture. There were so many clicks that you had to do, so many approvals to give, so many settings – basically, to upload a picture that took you a second to make, you had to go through minutes of endless clicking.

This obviously had to change. When users would continuously have to lose great amounts of time just to upload a picture, they would lose interest and stop posting altogether. Not to mention the headache that they got each time they had to go through that extremely confusing click rollercoaster.

So, to make the app more successful, they had to simplify it as much as possible. They had to ensure that people would not end up losing their patience on the first try. They had to make the process swift – with as few clicks as possible. This way, they would actually encourage people to post more, without them being afraid of the thought of losing a lot of time.

3. Ease of Sharing

Not only was Burbn very difficult when it came to uploading pictures, but it wasn't even easy to share the pictures with your family and friends. Not everyone had access to those pictures – and they had more chances of seeing them if you showed the picture right in their face.

Uploading and sharing took quite a lot of time and many roundabouts. While people were trying to "express a moment," to let the viewers enjoy the moment that they were currently living as well, the slow pace of Burbn did not allow them to do so. The fact that there were so many restrictions when it came to sharing also did not make matters any better. For an app that was so cluttered with fancy features, it was difficult to actually do something with it.

In the end, when the final result came through, everything was packed into their mission: to capture a moment and then share it to the world.

The First Filters

When Instagram originally had its launch, it was set apart from other apps thanks to their square pictures and their custom filters. In 2010, there weren't as many fancy cameras on phones – and even with the iPhone 4, as state-of-the-art as it may have been, it was still difficult to actually get a clear, expressive picture.

This is where filters came in. A well-made filter gave the possibility of turning an average picture into a professional-looking one. In a way, Systrom looks back at the first filters and agrees that this was likely what helped them take off with Instagram.

The first photo that was posted on Instagram was on July 16 of the year 2010, and it pictured a dog in Mexico, along with the foot of Systrom's girlfriend. This picture had been enhanced using the X-PRO2 filter – the first actual filter of Instagram.

After it was released on the iOS app store, Instagram really took off. Right now, the app features 23 filters – all of which have received classic names (e.g. Inkwell and Willow). This is quite a fancy difference since some of the names were actually inspired by Systrom's cocktail appreciation.

Instagram Immediate Hit Upon Launching

When Instagram was released to iOS on October 6, 2010, they thought the success would be slightly more successful than Burbn was – but what they did not expect was the success to be so great. In just one day, Instagram became the top picture sharing app that you could find for free on the app store.

In fact, Instagram got around 25,000 downloads in just one day. Even Systrom said that they did not expect the remarkable speed at which Instagram grew. They went from just a handful of users to the number one free photography app in just a couple of hours.

By the time the week came to an end, Instagram already gained around 100,000 users – which is four times more than it originally had. By the time the year also came to an end, the numbers went even higher. In only three months, in mid-December, Instagram already had one million users.

One could say that the success of the app was like a stroke of good luck. Since iPhone 4 with its quality camera was released in June 2010, it seemed to be like a great opportunity to socialize and share moments. This is why most people that had the latest iPhone could not miss on the opportunity to download the newest social media trend. Plus, considering that most of these people were already active users on Burbn, they would certainly not miss on the chance to check out the new social media app.

Many of those people were intrigued by the ease of use of the app, and the filters that you could use to make a picture look more professional. In a time when you needed countless hours to obtain that effect in Photoshop, Instagram made it just a matter of touching the screen (or a button). This product that they offered made Instagram very popular, and in a way, it was no wonder that the sales were going through the roof.

The strategies that they originally used would be what brought them success throughout time as well. First of all, the founders of Instagram tried to focus on what the people wanted – because after all, as a social media app, this was what mattered the most. Modifying and decluttering Burbn was actually the first complaint that they listened to – and its solution brought Instagram a fair amount of popularity. People were overjoyed of the fact that they did not have to waste a lot of time with uploads anymore.

Feedback for the developers was very important. With the users complaining of a problem, they would use this chance to actually begin fixing it. They used the feedback they received from Burbn, and they applied it to the new app. The first signups were people that already had a Burbn account – but eventually, the app started gaining more and more popularity – therefore, appearing on the top page of the app store.

The Decision to Sell to Facebook

At this point, with Instagram's success, you would be surprised that the app would be sold by the owners to Facebook. The decision to sell for about $1 billion caught many users by surprise, and they no longer knew what to expect from the platform. Would it be better compared to how it was before – or would it go downhill? Why would they decide to sell anyway?

Kevin Systrom, one of the Instagram founders, actually wrote a post where he explained exactly why he had to sell Instagram – and he said that it was only because he wanted what was best for the app. To quote Systrom, "Every day that passes, we see more experiences being shared through Instagram in ways that we never thought possible." In other words, they could see results when the app was on its own – but the moment it was acquired by Facebook, it gained even more popularity.

According to an interview they gave to the Wall Street Journal WSJ Magazine, they do not regret in the slightest that they sold Instagram for that sum – even though now it is worth at least 100 times that amount. In fact, one would say that their transaction is what brought Instagram so high up on the market.

passion and the desire to help. And for that, a few certain strategies should be in order.

Timeless Marketing Strategies

Whenever you are running a business – or planning to do so – you need to keep in mind that nothing can be done at random. You may be doing it out of passion – but in truth, you need to implement a lot of strategies there. You need to make sure that it has the potential to keep growing – that you give it the environment that it requires to keep growing.

Started by Mike Krieger and Kevin Systrom in 2010, the project did not seem to be such a big shot. Its previous version, Burbn, was actually a failed project – one that had to be dropped because it was unsuccessful.

Still, with failure, you may also reap success. This requires a lot of observation skill as well as a fair amount of marketing strategies. Instagram used three marketing strategies that can be used for any company – and which brought them a billion-dollar success.

Marketing Strategy 1: Focus on What People Want and Say – Listen for Demand

Think about it: when you are launching a business, you are doing so in the hopes of gaining some profit. You choose a line of business that seems to be attractive to the masses – because after all, you need to have demand. And once you find that line of business or the "it" that people are looking for, you start working it so that you can give it to the people.

The Importance of Feedback and Data Analysis

In the world of marketing, there is literally no room for guesswork. No matter if it is 2019 or 2010, if you are not driving your decisions based on feedback, then your edge has already been lost. If you wish to create an effective marketing campaign, the general rule is to listen to your audience and understand the basic factors:

- Who is your audience?
- What does your audience like?
- What does your audience need?
- When is your audience online and active?

If you do not have a clear picture of every aspect, there is no way that you can provide service that can solve their problems – and in the end, earn you money. You can't encourage a relationship with your client either, because there is no way for you to nurture them or offer them the solution that they need.

For you to do that and to avoid extinction simply because you are irrelevant to the market, you should carefully listen to what the people are saying. Focus on what they want, and this will allow you to be relevant to your cause.

You should also keep in mind a fairly popular saying, a Lee Resource stat that goes like this: "For every customer complaint there are 26 other unhappy customers who have remained silent." So, unless the user experience is particularly bad, people won't even bother to provide feedback on their experience. They will simply opt out of using your services ever again.

Plus, a lost customer is not generally the only casualty here. Generally speaking, a lost and dissatisfied customer is likely to share their unsatisfactory experience with at least eight other people. This is what happened with Burbn as well – people were not happy with the cluttered layout, and they ended up not recommending the app to their friends and family. Plus, with the way social media was continuously used, it was only a matter of time before the negative feedback would hurt their credibility.

Without good customer feedback, you will not be able to generate good customer loyalty. Users like to know that you care about their experience. Therefore, if you encourage your users to give you feedback, you may keep them engaged with your product.

The Market Research

Every professional in the industry will agree that before they launch a product on the market, they will have to do quite a fair amount of legwork. You do this to pick the interest of your customers and to keep them invested in your work. Without that legwork, you risk shooting blanks that will not reach anyone.

Your aim should be to find out what the people want by using various methods: surveys, social media feedback, test groups, and so on. If you notice a particular issue continuously popping up, you might want to address it and solve it.

You need to focus on what the people want so that you can offer them a deal that they cannot refuse. Try to find out exactly what they love from that particular app and see what approach you can take from that point on.

Even if a product has already been launched, you still need to listen to the voice of your people. You need to be aware of any demand for updates so that you may improve the customer experience. For example, while a product may have been working perfectly when it was originally launched, time will ask for certain improvements.

For example, let's say that a certain technology appeared that people seem to love. Or a certain trend makes people use certain features in apps in particular. If the masses begin to ask for that particular feature, you should be aware of the fact that they will not likely quit their requests. They will only grow stronger – and if you do not provide them exactly what they want, they will simply start looking somewhere else. They will look for another app and platform that will give them exactly what they want.

This is why it is imperative that you listen to the customer and create something that is committed to customer relationship and quality. Many business owners keep a great distance from the market, simply because they focus greatly on what they want as owners instead of focusing on what the people want. They fear that listening to the customers' opinion would change the company view forever.

However, by listening to the feedback, comments, and suggestions, you may be able to take a step forward. You should uncover the strengths of your company, and you should be able to serve the demand more efficiently. All this because you will know precisely what your users want.

What Instagram Did

Instagram developers heard what people were looking for. At that point, there were countless apps where people could share their location and send various pictures to their friend and family – but at the same time, the quality left to be desired. Those apps generally tried too much and focused on too many things – which eventually began to come back to them in a negative way. The original app, Burbn, started to become too cluttered – and people were no longer comfortable with using that social media platform.

At that point, Instagram started to "hear" what the masses were looking for: they wanted an app that they could use for sharing high-quality pictures. Granted, the location part of Burbn was fairly convenient sometimes – but after some close analysis, Krieger and Systrom realized that people were not necessarily using the location-sharing feature. However, they were using the photo sharing feature on a regular basis.

For this reason, originally, people started leaving Burbn and moving onto apps that were relatively easier to use. For the most part, they used picture-sharing features that had no complicated roundabouts. The Instagram developers almost immediately caught on to that, and they began on their plan to improve the customer experience.

Granted, they were fully aware that some of these changes would have to be drastic. Burbn was obviously flawed – and while they initially thought that "the more features, the merrier," they found out through the voice of their people that this was not actually something people were looking for.

As mentioned, most companies would stay away from the feedback received from customers in an attempt to keep the product the same way they initially viewed it. However, the developers of Instagram saw it otherwise: without the users, the app would no longer serve its purpose. This is why they carefully considered every request in order to solve the problem – and if this meant completely redesigning the product and changing the way in which it worked, then so be it.

Methods to Get Quality Feedback from Your Customers or Users

So, you decided that listening to the voice of your customers is worth the extra effort – but how do you do it? How do you actually listen to what they are saying, or focus on what they want so that you can actually improve their experience?

Well, here are some things that business owners tend to apply when they are at their startup – and for the most part, it works. When it comes to listening to what the people have to say, this can actually be very efficient for improving your marketing strategy.

Provide Live Chat Support

For someone to express their complaints regarding a service, they will need a way to communicate with the people in charge. Or if there aren't any actual complaints, the live chat can help answer some questions that the customer is having trouble with.

You can make the chat even more efficient by turning it into something proactive. For example, you may set for a live chat to appear when a user has been looking over the same page or post for a longer time – say 30 seconds. This will encourage the user to contact you and possibly provide feedback.

Offer a Dedicated Customer Feedback Form

You should provide at least one area or email where users can provide feedback. Users generally use it to provide complaints – but at the same time, they offer positive and constructive feedback. Instagram, for instance, created their help center particularly as a way to communicate better with their clients. They had this type of help center on Burbn as well, which helped them gather even more constructive feedback.

Use E-mail Surveys

Have you noticed how, as a Facebook and Instagram user, you keep getting many emails with what's happening on social media? For some people, this can be quite unnerving – but this email consistency is exactly what keeps your users in touch with you.

In these emails, Instagram and Facebook also attach surveys for the users to fill in. This way, they are able to get quality feedback so that they can continuously improve their services. They've done so in the past as well – and this is why Instagram is said to be worth more than $100 billion. They know exactly how to listen to the voices of the users.

Monitor the Social Channels

When a customer is unhappy about a product, the chances are very high that they will complain about it on social media. For instance, if the problem is Instagram, you will likely find someone complaining about it on Facebook or Twitter.

"Social listening" may require a fair number of tools and a significant amount of time indeed. But generally speaking, if a customer is unhappy but does not provide email feedback, the chances are very high that they will complain about it on other social media platforms. In the end, if you do not have the tools, you might want to try collaborating with the website.

In a way, Instagram selling to Facebook provided them better access to the social channels. So, now they can get data that was out of their reach in the past – making it much easier for them to monitor feedback and listen to the voice of the people.

Use Polls

Polls are very efficient when it comes to collecting data and feedback from users – which is why you should not overlook their worth. The good part is that polls can also be added through advertisement, making it nearly unnoticeable for the user.

For example, every now and again, Instagram adds a poll as a sponsored link. Those that are interested may access those polls and answer the question in the way they see it fit, On the other hand, if they are not particularly interested in answering the poll, they can always scroll down and go over the poll.

The Voice of People Is Important

To put it as simple as possible, listening to what the users of your service have to say is quite important. They will tell you exactly what is wrong with what you are "selling" (no matter if it's a product or a service), and you will know what you should do in order to fix it.

Instagram developers, for instance, were very proactive. They listened to the complaints of their users – and saw that more and more of them were leaving Burbn for other applications that were much easier to use. The problem here was that people wanted to take great pictures, and then share them with their friends and family. It took an entire rebranding and remodeling of the original business, but the people from Instagram actually did it.

Marketing Strategy 2: Solve a Real Problem – Fill the Demand – Supply

Now that you know what people are complaining about, it's time to be proactive. You need to find the problem, and then try to solve it as quickly as possible. You need to fill the demand and begin supplying to your users.

For some people, this might be easier said than done. Where do you start? Do you only need to retouch some issues – or do you have to rebuild completely? Well, in this stage, you need to figure out what you have to do.

In a way, you could say that a problem is actually an opportunity in disguise. You get to see exactly what is wrong with a business based on feedback or whatever means you have. After that, you follow a set of steps to fill in that demand. With this strategy, you have to take a rather systematic approach – and while it may not prevent you from experiencing problems in the future, it will give you the tools you need to stop this situation in its path.

Basic Steps to Solve a Problem and Fill Demand

For that, there are a few steps that you might want to follow in order to solve a problem and fill in the demand.

1. Define the Problem

As expected, in order to properly solve a problem, you have to define it first. This is usually started in the first marketing strategy, where you listen to the feedback of those using your services. however, in this stage, you try to define what the most important problem is – and then you go forward with that one instead of addressing any concerns that are irrelevant.

In the case of Instagram, the problem was that taking and uploading pictures was quite a difficult task to do. You had to stock them in your phone first, edit them manually (most people using Photoshop and other editing programs), and after which you uploaded them on Instagram. The entire process was fairly troublesome, and many people opted against it altogether simply because they did not want to go through the entire ordeal.

This caused many users to go for other social media websites and apps just to make things easier for themselves. They wanted to easily share a picture with their friends and family, and not spend the entire day going through endless clicks.

2. Dissect the Problem

Depending on the problem, you need to analyze the way in which it affects your business. Is it because of a specific situation, only affecting you on the short term – or is it because of a more pressing situation that affects your business in the long term? Is the problem confined to just one person – or is it widespread to more than a few people?

In Instagram's case, it was fairly obvious that the problem was in the long term. People wanted easier methods to post a picture – and the way in which Burbn functioned at that point did not make things any easier for them. The problem there involved more than one person – which could be seen from the way people were leaving the platform.

After the problem was dissected, they needed to find a way in which people could post pictures much faster. They included as many variables in their analysis so that they could further improve the customer experience.

3. Start Making Decisions

So, at this point, you found the problem and successfully analyzed it. With that settled, now you have to set a course of action. In this stage, you have to identify what your priorities are. Do you want to keep going the way you are, to follow the same path of your business that you've been following until now – or are you willing to make some changes to make the experience even better?

For instance, when Instagram was originally Burbn, the main focus was on location sharing – and less on the picture sharing aspect. The developers focused on the ease of sharing a status or location – but when it came to sharing a picture, people had to go through a series of inconveniencing steps.

As a result, they made the decision that instead of making a location-sharing app, they should make one that shares high-quality pictures. Plus, these pictures would have to be posted quickly – because after all, Instagram was all about sharing a moment and a place.

So, how did they decide to do that? Well, the answer to that was fairly simple: instead of storing a picture in the phone memory before posting it, they decided that the quickest way would be to take the picture through the app directly. This way, there would no longer be a need for endless roundabouts whenever you simply wanted to post a basic picture.

What was crucial at that point was that they decluttered the app of anything that was not necessary. The problem at that point was that Burbn was trying to be too many things at once, which only seemed to confuse its users. This is why they decided to set some "clean" grounds where the main focus was on picture sharing.

Plus, another feature that they decided to add was that of filters. This way, instead of having to edit the pictures themselves, people could simply choose a filter of their liking while taking the picture – and soon enough, they should be able to post the picture for their friends and family to see.

Instagram's purpose here was to give the users exactly what they wanted – not what they wanted them to want. If this means changing from a location-sharing app to a photo-sharing one, then that was the way the cookie crumbled.

4. Analyze the Problem-Solving Strategy

In most cases, the first solution that comes into your mind is not always the best one to go for. Similarly, the strategy that you think about the most is not always the best one either.

Ideally, you should make a list of solutions that you could implement, listing all the pros and cons. This way, you will be able to get a clear image over what you should do to make the business work.

This decision was certainly not easy for the developers of Instagram. Practically, in order to implement the strategies that they wanted, they first had to shut down the entire Burbn project. This was something huge for them.

Moreover, the way in which they had to "regroup" would also be affected. At that point, they functioned based on statuses posts and location-sharing – but with the redevelopment, the main focus would be on picture sharing. What if it didn't catch on? What if they would be able to retain more popularity if they kept on with the location-sharing part?

Granted, there were a lot of pros and cons that they had to consider – but this was a risk that they had to be willing to take. After all, things were not changing for the better the way it was – and considering that the user experience was also quite troublesome, a choice had to be made.

5. Choose the Best Solution

You've given some significant thought to this, and have analyzed all the pros and cons. However, in order to fill in the demand, you have to choose the option that is best suited for your profit. Not only does it need to bring you more profit, but it also has to bring clients to the table.

Once you have laid the groundwork, think about what the optimal solution would be. Bear in mind that no solution is likely to be foolproof – but if you use logic and clarity while avoiding acting in a rash manner, you are likely to make a decision that will benefit anyone that is involved.

Other Instagram Strategies to Solve a Problem and Fill the Demand

Instagram was fairly productive when it came to strategies – and this did not involve only the stage after Burbn was shut down. The customization continued for the good of the company, and from a random app made by a person that loves coding, it turned out to be a billion-dollar purchase. Here are the strategies that were implemented to make it so successful.

1. They only focused on one thing

Generally speaking, when you try to do many things at once, you end up gaining average results because you tend to be all over the place. Some people are fairly good at multitasking – but the average person cannot succeed in too many things at once. This is why we specialize in a certain career during our lifetime – because no one can really excel by trying to be too many things.

When Instagram first came into being as Burbn, this is exactly what it was doing: trying to be too many things at once. It was used for posting status updates, check-in, pictures, and many other things. The app itself was cluttered, which is why it ended up taking such a long time to load. You also needed to go through a variety of clicks just to go through a single task.

The problem was that neither of these tasks was truly developed to its finest point. All of them were average because the coding was done for all features at once. This is why they realized that the best course here was not to be average in everything – but to be the best in just one aspect.

But which one to choose? This one was also obvious. People loved taking pictures everywhere they went. Plus, with the recent release of the iPhone 4, whose camera amazed everyone, they decided that the best course would be to optimize the app for better picture support. They took down everything else, cleaned the app of clutter, and made picture-sharing the main feature of Instagram.

2. They optimized for Android

When Instagram originally came out, it was only optimized for iOS – meaning that you could only use it if you had an iPhone. All Android users could do was watch their friends post pictures and use cool filters while standing next to them.

After a few weeks, there were more than 30,000 million users on Instagram – and all of them were iPhone users.

Eventually, Android also began to take up speed on the market – and Instagram developers saw it as an opportunity. They began coding the app for Android so that they could release it on the market – bringing Instagram to millions of other users.

Granted, the entire process took quite some time. It took a little under two years until the application was available for Android users as well – but once that plan was put into motion, it took off fairly quickly. There was an increasing demand for Instagram to be made available on Android platforms – and Instagram developers made it possible. This way, they would manage to fill a demand and gain even more users. Granted, by the time it was released, Instagram had more than 5 million downloads in just 6 days.

3. They optimized for upload on other social media websites

When Instagram came out, Facebook and Twitter were already going strong. These websites were very popular – and anyone who wanted to have a social presence would have a Facebook account. It was all the rage at that time.

The problem with Facebook was that while it could post pictures, videos, and other interesting stuff, it did not have the filters that Instagram had. The pictures on Instagram looked nice, fancy and professional – whereas the pictures on other social media websites looked plain and average.

There was one demand on the market – and that came from the people that were using social media websites. Several people that were using Facebook were asking for the editing features that Instagram had. They wanted to post fabulous pictures on Facebook as well, with the same ease.

While the developers of Instagram could not exactly do anything about the basic Facebook coding and filters, they did make it so that its users could share on the more popular social media platforms. This way, if someone took a cute picture of themselves on Instagram, they could easily share it on Facebook, Tumblr, or Foursquare as well.

By integrating with other social media websites, Instagram gained even more popularity. Many people who did not have an Instagram until that point had downloaded it just so that they could take advantage of the filters. Todd Warren, a venture capitalist, also explained the benefits that this strategy brought in an article meant for Forbes:

> "The social nature of the activity was a natural generator for new people to enter the network and download the application. The attachment to existing social networks provided a very cost-effective channel strategy. Their sales strategy was about seeding the social network effectively to get additional adoption."

Simply put, despite the fact that it wanted to create its own community, Instagram did not try to separate the people from the existent platforms. Instead, they tried to "mingle". They refrained from trying to modify the existent social behavior – and gave the people exactly what they wanted.

Instead of limiting them to only their platform, Instagram allowed them to spread their wings – all while using their platform as a medium.

4. They made it simpler to use

They did make it so that pictures were the main focus on Instagram – but only with that change, it was no guarantee that the app would be very easy to use. This is why they decided that the best course before launching would be to take away all the clutter and make the app relatively easy to navigate.

The success of the app might be attributed to change, in a way – because it was eventually picked up by high-profile individuals. Its popularity attracted a number of influencers which brought Instagram even more to the top. And you didn't even have to do anything too complicated: just snap a picture, choose a filter, and show the world how good you are at taking professional pictures – even though you took them with a hand-me-down phone.

The secret for this second cycle of the strategy is to know exactly what the demand is. You have to know precisely what people want so that you can configure the app accordingly. This way, when you launch it, you will know for certain that the product you created will get quite a lot of success.

In Instagram's case, the biggest problem was the way pictures were handled. People found the entire process to be rather troublesome, and they proceeded to fix that issue, along with a few other tweaks. They lowered the barrier, and eventually, made it much simpler to take a good picture that they could share with their friends and family.

Marketing Strategy 3: Launch Small and Develop Based on Feedback

Those working in the marketing world already know the drill. Once you have launched your product, it feels natural to simply wipe your hands of the process and simply head home. Since the hard part is over and you have been launched, all you have to do is sit back and wait for results.

That is both true and false. Indeed, the hard part is over – but you aren't exactly done. The launch is only the first step of your journey – but it is by no means the end. At this point, you are starting with a cycle of listening to the voice of the users, learning from what they say, iterating everything, and shipping possible improvements based on what they told you.

This is part of why Instagram was actually so successful. Unlike other brands that went around it their own way, they had a certain method of dealing with things – and that was to listen to what the masses had to say. The product was launched – but work still had to be done. This is why 1/3 of the mobile users in the US have Instagram – simply because the developers' drive for improvement appealed to the masses.

Launching Small vs. Launching Big

Many companies tend to do this: they spend years trying to develop a product – and after a long time has already passed, they decide to launch. This product will contain everything they believe the users will like – so, all that is left to do is to just sit back and watch. In their eyes, the product is complete – and they believe that this big launch will have everything that the user will need to have a great experience.

The emphasis here will be on the word "believe." The problem is that when they develop the product, they do so based on what they *think* will work – but the user might have a completely different opinion. When you launch big, the product is likely to be final in the eyes of the developer – but for the users, it might either end up being too cluttered or lacking several important features.

If you think about it carefully, Burbn was exactly this way. When it was originally developed, the developers thought that the final product, the "big launch" should have as many features as possible. However, when people started to complain or leave the website, they eventually realized that "less is more."

This is why, when they closed Burbn, they decided that a big launch should no longer be their target. Instead, they made a small launch for a small product – an MVP which they decided to improve continuously after it was launched.

Simply put, they launched a basic app that only took a few weeks to develop – and once they started receiving feedback, they improved the app based on the user feedback. This is practically the reason why we still see constant updates in the app store.

What Happens Once You Spike?

When it comes to handling a business, regardless of its nature, the perspective generally comes from the way you break down every role in your marketing team. Your team should have four core responsibilities that will take you through the marketing funnel – with the launch touching upon the first three stages.

1. **Reach:** Try to get the message in front of the correct audience. For instance, when Instagram came through, the intended group was 18-44 years of age. This was a success for Instagram, as statistics show that 31% of the users are aged 18-24, 32% are aged 25-34, and 16% are aged 35-44.
2. **Attract:** Get your audience to use your product so that they become leads. Instagram was fairly lucky in this aspect, as various users were actually celebrities or influencers. These people would bring even more people to Instagram, which would raise the popularity of the website even more.
3. **Convert:** Convince the leads to sign up and become users. Instagram had a very attractive thing to offer – and that was filters. Thanks to this, they could post professional-looking pictures without spending countless hours on programs such as Photoshop.
4. **Educate:** This generally occurs after the launch – but here, you enable the users to get great value from

the product that you offered them. Instagram allowed not only for high-quality pictures, but the rest of Instagram's content also proved to be of general interest for the masses.

The launch will create a boost in the traffic that will be great when you look through the "reach" and "spike" in perspective. However, when you go deeper, things will no longer look as cheery. Truth be told, a product launch is not generally highly targeted. Granted, it does lead to record traffic days. However, the bulk that matters is generated by those who actually buy or use your product – not just "visit" it.

Everyone is curious about a new product – and they are bound to stick around for a while to see how it turns out. However, without proper monitoring and maintenance, once the spike ends, the product will return to normal levels – and no one can really say how it will affect the traffic.

Take, for instance, Instagram. After it has been launched, it had more than 1 million users in only 24 hours. However, those users may have signed up only out of curiosity, to see exactly what the deal with this new app was. They can hang around for a while – but if they get bored or see that they do not have anything of interest there, the chances are very high that they will simply drop their account and go for other social media platforms.

The Post-Launch Feedback

Once the product has been launched, the job of the product market is to identify the issues or confusion that might stop the people from using the product. A few useful steps would be the following:

1. Listen to the Unfiltered Responses

When a product is launched, you are likely to get quite a lot of feedback – both qualitative and quantitative. You need to keep in mind that not all the reviews will be positive; some of them might cause quite a lot of burn in the beginning. What you have to do is listen without any negative reactions – and treat is as constructive feedback.

Most of the time, you will realize that the greatest issue here is not related to the actual product – but to everything that surrounds it. This is why you need to collect as much feedback as you possibly can – both from those working with you, as well as from those who are using the product.

2. Decipher the Feedback

You've gathered the feedback – but now you also need to make sense of it. Once you have all the required opinions from those who have become familiarized with the product, you should also try to organize that feedback. Figure out what the main complaints are and put them into categories.

For example, some complaints on Instagram might be that there aren't enough filters, or that it still takes quite a long time until you post the picture in the dimensions that you want. Your job as a product developer would be to take all that feedback and to use it in a constructive manner. This way, you will be able to provide the users exactly what they need from your product.

3. Continuously Ship

When it comes to software, engineers continuously have to ship improvements to the way their coding works. The same thing happens when it comes to product marketing. Instead of spending lots of money on a re-launch, the best way to gain success would be to find small solutions regularly – providing maintenance as often as you can.

Instagram is once more a very good example here. When Burbn came out, the owners did not make as many changes to its interface. Eventually, to make it in the way that the users wanted it to, they had to drop the Burbn project and re-launch it as Instagram.

At that point, a lesson was learned. Instead of trying to do everything all at once, the developers decided that the best way would be to start with a basic platform – and then continuously work their magic from there. Granted, the Initial Instagram app was fairly good – but by providing continuous updates, they would no longer have to redesign so much that would require a re-launch. It is less time consuming, and it will be all the more profitable.

In most cases, baby steps are recommended after launching a product – but make sure that they are also thoughtful. It might be very tempting to create a well-developed product and leave it like that. Still, as a marketer, you shouldn't remove your foot from the pedal the moment you successfully launched.

In the end, it is always best to launch small — starting with a basic product that people might enjoy. After that, you should gather as much feedback as possible. The big launch will eventually happen as well — but it will be in a way that you know for certain the users will enjoy. No one gets it right from the first try.

Conclusion

When you are managing your own company, it is understandable that you want to get fast results on a project that you have been working on for quite some time. However, generally speaking, all it takes is a good idea and some careful strategizing. Look at Instagram – who knew that a simple love for coding would end up being such a success on social media? The founders probably never even thought that their idea would end up being worth billions of dollars.

Granted, the journey was not easy. In the beginning, it even ended in failure – and they had to shut down the project altogether. Even so, they did not give up – but instead, they learned from their mistakes. Through their failure, they realized that certain things had to be done in order to reap success. This actually managed to motivate them even more.

In the end, they re-launched, rebranded, and recreated everything. Instagram was no longer used to share locations – but it became the number one photo sharing app. The idea was simple, as was the layout – but the fact that the pictures had the highest quality made it priceless in the eyes of the users. Moreover, no other social media platform had the filters that Instagram brought to the table.

It might not come out the way you wanted from the very start – but each project you may have will eventually be successful, provided you offer it the appropriate attention. Think about any business or project idea that you have: how do you think these timeless ideas will help you progress?

When you have answered that, what will you do to get eyeballs on your project? And how will you turn those eyeballs into leads, customers, and raving fans?

One way is to market your project on Instagram, or any other social media site. That's super effective if it's done correctly.

Unfortunately, most of the advice about social media marketing is based on metric-chasing-myths.

In our next book, *Likes Don't Pay Bills*, we bust the five most significant social media marketing myths so that you can win on social media.

If you don't want to buy that book now, but you're interested in getting up to date marketing tactics and strategies every month right to your inbox, consider signing up to our monthly marketing email.

Visit sunbirdmarketing.com